the
BEST
death

Dr Sarah Winch is head of the Medical Ethics, Law and Professionalism discipline at the Faculty of Medicine, University of Queensland. She is also the CEO of Health Ethics Australia, a charity that aims to improve death literacy for everyone and compassion awareness for clinicians. She teaches healthcare ethics and researches end-of-life care. Sarah's professional health ethics advice is sought nationally and internationally by clinicians and government agencies. A widely published author, she draws on her expertise and experiences in end-of-life healthcare to help others get the best death possible.

All proceeds from the sale of this book will be donated to the charity Health Ethics Australia.

First published 2017 by University of Queensland Press
PO Box 6042, St Lucia, Queensland 4067 Australia

uqp.com.au
uqp@uqp.uq.edu.au

Cover design by Christabella Designs
Typeset in 12/16 pt Bembo Std by Post Pre-press Group, Brisbane
Printed in Australia by McPherson's Printing Group, Melbourne

National Library of Australia Cataloguing-in-publication data is available at
http://catalogue.nla.gov.au

ISBN 978 0 7022 5972 2 (pbk)
ISBN 978 0 7022 5937 1 (pdf)
ISBN 978 0 7022 5938 8 (epub)
ISBN 978 0 7022 5939 5 (kindle)

This book is not intended as a substitute for the medical advice of physicians.
Please consult with a medical professional for advice regarding your health
concerns.

UQP is not responsible for content found on non-UQP websites.

University of Queensland Press uses papers that are natural, renewable
and recyclable products made from wood grown in sustainable forests.
The logging and manufacturing processes conform to the environmental
regulations of the country of origin.

the BEST death

SARAH WINCH

UQP

contents

For Brandon, Emma and Zoe Winch. Love always.

dying well

In 2008, I sat next to my husband, Lincoln, in a small Brisbane hospital. He was a work-to-live sort of guy, always ready with a joke and a laugh; a laconic, larrikin Australian who excelled at sport. Lincoln realised he was likely to die that night, and he did, around 4 am the next morning; the traditional 'death hours'. His cause of death was recorded as kidney cancer. Discovered just four months previously, it had been there for a long while as it had spread throughout his body. He had no idea. Nothing had seemed the matter, just a few initial odd niggly aches and pains, but he was still relatively young at 48 years of age and presumably fit.

How wrong can you be? Very, as it turns out.

Experience, as they say, is the best teacher. Although I am not dead, or dying imminently as far as I am aware (but I know death can be sneaky), I seem to have spent most of my working life connected to the dying and their carers. I am a clinical ethicist, researcher, nurse and educator with decades of expertise in death and dying whose professional knowledge was being tested in the most personal and painful way. Driving home alone, early on that Saturday morning, I thought of the many deaths I had seen; Lincoln's was one of the most peaceful, pain free and comfortable. He would have been pleased. He always was competitive!

Lincoln's death is a good news death story, if one can say that exists. He wasn't writhing in agony, screaming incomprehensibly, rigid with fear or cursing the gods. It was as 'good' as we could hope and plan for. He had incredible pain but it was managed with the usual techniques that modern medicine can supply. He exercised what limited control he had over his disease in terms of accepting and rejecting treatments. He had a clear plan for how his death should happen based on the values he had cultivated and lived by, and importantly, how he would spend his time preceding death. Just as in life, he had the death thing sorted.

A few days before he died, Lincoln asked me to write about his experience. He knew the type of death he wanted, but I knew how to make it happen based on years of experience. He thought this combination helped him achieve the end of life he desired – the 'best death possible' for him. If he was going to die, then he was definitely going to be in charge, all the way. All things considered, his dying days had turned out well, and he urged me to write about his story so others could benefit. 'Who would know any of this stuff?' he said. I agreed to write this book. It was a deathbed promise made without any comprehension about how difficult a task this was to become. A grieving author combined with a death-averse publishing and bookselling industry do not make for encouraging conditions for writing about dying to the general public. My first book, *Best Death Possible: A Guide to Dying in Australia*, was self-published with help from supportive colleagues. It met a huge need in the community and has led to this expanded and improved volume with a publisher who is comfortable talking about dying and an author who still has plenty to say.

How it all began

Returning from a 'holiday of a lifetime' in New York City in early December 2007, Lincoln felt decidedly unwell. This was unusual for him. He thought he had caught a virus on the flight home. A visit to his doctor resulted in tests showing the calcium in his blood was very high. We were told to immediately find out what was causing the problem. The news was not good – in fact it was catastrophic. Scans showed cancer throughout Lincoln's abdomen. The origin was probably his kidney, but it was everywhere, including his lungs. A cure was not available and there were few treatments. His doctor thought he had approximately two weeks to live. He survived four months.

We were poleaxed. The doctor breaking the news used the term 'mind-fuck' to describe how we must be feeling. I was taken aback by the language and was thinking furiously about what else must be the cause. There must have been a mix-up with the pathology reports. This happens more often than it should. Soon, we would get a phone call apologising for this dreadful mistake, which we would graciously accept, and get back to our real lives. This new life was surreal and horrible. This was Lincoln we were talking about. We had presumed he was in good physical condition. He loved to exercise. Fitness and healthy living were his passions. He lifted weights daily. He ran four times per week; his times in 2007 had been the best he had achieved in a long time. He also cycled about 100 kilometres per week. Admittedly, that had become harder (secondaries covering the bottom third of each lung will have that effect) but he put it down to being the oldest in the group and less frequent training. There was no history of cancer in his family of any type; he did not smoke and rarely drank alcohol. He loved life, was happy and was particularly enjoying this stage of his life.

Lincoln was admitted to hospital and given an infusion to bring his blood calcium down to normal levels. The next day we were told he could leave after the doctor had reviewed his test results. As the day progressed we were keen to go home. Our situation was starting to make sense. There was no mistake involved in his pathology reports. It was true. Lincoln had cancer, all through him. He could not live for much longer and did not want to be sitting around in hospital. We asked the nurse when the doctor would see the test results. The answer was disappointing: not until he arrived that evening. Only then would we get permission to leave the hospital. This did not suit us at all. The nurse was perplexed. 'Why are you in such a hurry?' she inquired. 'Don't you like it here?' Well, no, quite frankly, we did not. It was not personal, but in our minds, when you are 48 years old and have just been given a diagnosis of terminal cancer you don't want to spend the precious hours you have left in hospital, waiting for the doctor to swing past. I offered to ring the doctor for her with the results. This galvanised the nurse into action. There was no need for me to ring the doctor; she would be able to do it herself. Lincoln's blood calcium had come down and we went home.

This incident taught us a couple of valuable lessons. First, health professionals generally rely on their own customs and practices that may not suit the dying person. Fortunately, these may be able to be negotiated pleasantly to suit all parties. Second, and more importantly, Lincoln hated being in hospital. He was always looking for the quickest way out. This gave us some initial clues about the type of treatment he was going to tolerate and the best place to give him the care that he needed.

Once home we started to do some research via the internet. Lincoln had Kidney Cancer Stage 4. It was extremely serious, but we noted twenty per cent of patients had been known to survive for five years. Wow! That sounded fantastic. Two weeks versus five years; we'll take it! We would aim for surviving five years. After all, how many patients were as fit as Lincoln? He had stopped running, as it was a little uncomfortable with the tumours, but kept riding and lifting weights. He increased his visits to the gym and started a serious relationship with the rowing machine. We began to plan a life where he retired, kept as fit as possible, stayed out of hospital and lived for another five years.

We were sorted and on track. This lasted a week before Lincoln suddenly started seeing in double. A brain scan confirmed four more cancer tumours. The cancer really was everywhere. Lincoln could not watch television or read. Driving with brain tumours is not the best idea so that had to stop as well. This produced a double whammy to Lincoln's independence and quality of life. We had thought he may be in the lucky twenty per cent of patients who survived five years, but what shape were they in? Did they have to spend most of that time going to and from a hospital, waiting for results, not being able to see, or not in control of their bodily functions?

Time to consider plan 'B' or, more aptly, 'D' for death and dying. We desperately wanted as long a life as possible, but began to prepare for Lincoln dying – just in case. Our plans reflected Lincoln's personality; his likes and dislikes. He wanted to stay in control and maintain a high level of functioning. He hated hospital, preferring to ride with his mates, or spend time with the family. He thought about the best place to die and asked me what it was like to die in a physical sense. Logically, given Lincoln's dislike of hospitals, dying at home was preferable. We contacted our local hospice service and decided on a preferred hospital as a backup. It needed to be close, quiet, with easy parking. We wanted experienced nursing staff who understood the needs of the dying person and their family.

In a matter of weeks Lincoln's fit abdomen expanded with fluid. He felt very uncomfortable and a trip to the hospital was needed to drain the fluid. This was successful but it returned and was relentless. Lincoln commented in his notes: 'Now continually filled with fluid and need to be drained. Maybe 7–8 litres drained over two weeks. Feel very uncomfortable and do not have any appetite at all. Spent the week in hospital laid up and discharged with no energy at all.' He could not stand for long, or walk more than a few steps. The fluid kept coming and now filled one of Lincoln's lungs.

His abdominal tumours began to block his gut, causing him to vomit. We went to hospital to control the sick feeling and drain the fluid in the lung. At this point, Lincoln decided his quality of life, as he defined it, was seriously eroded. He would not be accepting further treatment, including further drainage of the fluid. He wanted to be comfortable. He was preparing to die in hospital and would not be returning home. Lincoln was approaching death. He died peacefully a few days later, just six weeks before his 49th birthday.

How to use this book

I have written this book for you. If you or a loved one are facing the worst news possible, it will help you clarify your thoughts, wishes and actions as the dying person or as their carer. I use Lincoln's story to introduce you to useful techniques that can guide end-of-life conversations, planning and decision making. For a broader perspective I have also included the stories of others. You can find the information you need quickly, by looking at the contents page, or reading from start to finish. In general, I have written to speak directly to the dying, but carers are critically important. This book is for them as well.

In my time as a health professional I have seen, and continue to see, many sad stories. Now I have lived through one. Lincoln trusted me to help him gain the peaceful death he sought. To do this we needed to navigate through what he jokingly called 'Sarah's world' – the healthcare space: a jumble of service providers, treatments, research and education. I wrote this because I promised Lincoln I would. He wanted me to share this knowledge in a practical way, so that you can get the best death possible for yourself or your loved one on your terms.

This book is for adults. While I am considered experienced in my field, it only provides general guidance.

For specific advice that takes into account your situation, please consult a member of your health team. You will find prompts throughout the book to check in with both your healthcare team and your carers.

CHAPTER 1

are you living the last
12 months of your life?

Understanding bad news

Like us, when you first hear the diagnosis of 'no cure', you are likely to experience numbness and disbelief. That may be where you are at right now. When we received our news, Lincoln actually pinched me in case he was dreaming. When I yelped and glared at him, he abandoned that strategy. Perhaps you think: 'I can live with no cure, as long as I can put off death for a while.' This may be the case, but what does it mean for managing the end of your life or that of your loved one? *How can you get the best death possible when you are finding it hard to believe that your death is going to be sooner than expected?*

Many people put thoughts of death out of their mind. A common refrain is: 'Why worry about dying when I could be hit by a bus and be gone tomorrow?' While some experience sudden death, most people do not. They actually see the bus approaching that is going to hit them some time in the coming weeks or months. Death is never easy but there are advantages in knowing it is on its way. You can put your 'house in order', complete your bucket list, and reflect on how you have lived your life and on what your death should be like.

To start this process you can:

- take steps to believe the news

- tell others and learn how to manage their reactions

- do some simple research

- understand the difference between diagnosis, prognosis and the experience of illness.

Believing bad news

Believing a diagnosis of 'no cure' can be very difficult. This is true if you have just found out about your illness or if you have been receiving treatment for a while and were hoping for a cure. Some people do not want to be told. For others, the truth is a relief, confirming what they have felt for some time. Ideally, your healthcare team will break the news in stages, gently, so the person who is receiving the news can assimilate what they are being told. Most probably, they will repeat it several times. They will need to. In the meantime, if you are having trouble moving out of the dream state of unbelief, the following techniques may help.

Techniques to help you believe bad news

1. If possible, take a relative or friend to your medical appointment. They can confirm what you think the doctor is saying and support you afterwards. Try not to pinch them – they will probably be in shock as well.

2. Repeat back to the doctor or nurse what they have told you. Our conversations with the doctor went like this: 'So Lincoln has kidney cancer that has spread all through his body and there is no treatment? Is that what you are saying?' The doctor confirmed this. We repeated: 'There is no treatment available, no chemotherapy or radiotherapy?' He agreed this was the case.

3. Write down information and check the waiting room for leaflets or fact sheets relevant to your situation.

4. Read your notes and your information several times and try to absorb the meaning.

5. Write down any questions.

6. At your next visit confirm what the doctor has told you and ask your questions.

7. Ask the doctor if you can record their responses. This may not be permitted by some doctors but it is

worth asking. If you do get permission, many smart phones have this capability. An old-fashioned tape recorder will also do the job. This will help you as you can replay the recording at your convenience.

8. Understanding is complicated further if English is not your first language. This is because in times of stress your ability to understand and communicate may falter. In this case request an interpreter. If one is not available take a support person who is fluent in both languages to your next visit so that communication can proceed as smoothly as possible.

9. You may like to do some research. The internet is a great source of information but not all of it is accurate. Anyone can post information that may or may not be true. Despite this, I believe the good outweighs the bad. There are reputable sites maintained by major health institutions, governments or organisations that represent people who have a particular disease; for example, the Cancer Council or Alzheimer's Australia. If you find information that concerns you, discuss it with your doctor or nursing team.

10. If you are the carer or support person, allow the dying person some time on their own to deal

with their feelings. Understandably, there is a lot of emotion to process as well as information to absorb. Sometimes being on your own helps (both for you and the carer).

11. Start acting on the information even if it feels unreal. Develop short-term goals. These can be simple things like getting legal matters sorted, organising a power of attorney or writing your will.

12. If your condition permits, take some light exercise, such as walking.

13. Importantly, try to do as much as possible, for as long as you can. A diagnosis of 'incurable' or 'terminal illness' does not mean that you are dying tomorrow. Life is still for living – even more so in these situations.

If you are not sure about your situation, but you suspect your condition is terminal, ask your doctor or nurse the following question:

Do you think I will be alive in twelve months?

This gives your healthcare team scope to acknowledge and discuss what they may be thinking. It opens up a conversation that moves from living with an illness to living the last twelve months of your life.

While this is confronting and devastating, it does mean you have time to put a number of things in action. Some need to be done more quickly than others, but we will get to those shortly. Some may be things that you want to do at a personal level – your bucket list. These are things you want to do before you 'kick' the bucket, so to speak. Lincoln had a 'reverse bucket list' – things he never wanted to do again, including going back to work!

Telling others and managing reactions

Once you are sure about your information you may want to tell others. This can be exhausting. We wanted to keep people informed but hated repeating the story over and over again. Here are some tips to help you communicate with friends and family.

Tips for telling others

1. Keep people informed to the extent you think is manageable. The time you have left is now yours to spend wisely. You may not want to talk on the phone all evening, reporting the latest test results to friends and family. Explain this to them.

2. Keep the message simple and repeat it.

3. Nominate a trusted 'official messenger' who can relay the news to others on your behalf.

4. Accept that friends may be sad and emotional, but let them deal with it in their own way.

5. Accept offers of help and care from others. You will need it.

6. Do not accept blame or poor behaviour from others. One message conveyed to me was: 'Sarah was a nurse – why didn't she pick up on Lincoln's cancer?' This type of interaction is truly not helpful and you should ignore it, like I did!

Doing research

If this is a new diagnosis you will probably want to use the internet to find out as much as you can. Despite being the director of a research unit in a large Queensland hospital, I did not use the hospital computers to look up the medical literature regarding kidney cancer. I was very tempted but decided to trust our doctor and leave the cancer medicine to him. I knew he had an excellent reputation. However, I did want to know what was likely to happen at a personal level, and what we needed to plan for, and for that I used the internet.

The Google queen

Google is a wonderful search engine for all sorts of things, including end-of-life care and decision making. When I type in 'end of life care' as a search term, I get over nine million responses in half a second. There is a huge amount of information on the internet. One of the most important websites for you to look at is maintained by Palliative Care Australia (see Appendix 2). Click through the different sections that apply to you. There are also many printed brochures available to help you understand all aspects of palliative care.

I found patient blogs interesting. These are patients' stories about their treatments that can be found on the internet. Just after Lincoln was diagnosed he was offered a drug that had been approved for use but was not subsidised in Australia at that time. The drug information listed what appeared to be every known side effect in medicine. It left us totally confused. I decided to check patients' experiences from taking this drug in other countries, as described by them in their blogs. They were 'warts and all' stories but gave us a good idea of what we could possibly expect and some of them did identify the same side effects that Lincoln experienced.

taking care when using the internet

One of the great benefits of the internet is also its greatest drawback – it is uncensored. In terms of patient blogs this means you will read good stories, bad ones and some that may cause fear and anxiety. Be aware of this and be careful! Monitor your reaction and if you are distressed, then avoid reading any more blogs. You can turn the computer off. On the other hand, if you want to more fully understand people's experiences who have the same illness and are facing death, then the internet is a rich source of information. Their experience is not likely to be exactly the same as yours, but it may be useful to know when considering unusual treatments.

Understanding the language

Lincoln was diagnosed only a short time before he died but he had advantages over some people who become suddenly terminally ill. He had me! Or more precisely, my knowledge of the healthcare system and a basic understanding of the treatment of cancer, including the language used. If you are unsure about the medical terms being used, ask your doctor to explain them to you. If you need more help, MedicineNet has a useful dictionary called MedTerms™ or you may like to try the Medical Dictionary (see Appendix 2). Type in what you want to know and the answer will be provided. These cannot replace the advice of your doctor or others in the treating team but may help you understand more when you are discussing your treatment with them.

If you do not have internet access, a friend or family member may be able to help you. Most local libraries in Australia also have computers where you can access the internet and classes to help you get started. These are popular. You may need to book a time at your local library.

Understanding 'diagnosis'

Your diagnosis or diagnoses are important terms that tell you what is going wrong with your body and what to expect in terms of how you will manage your disease. Sometimes your treating team will not know exactly how things started and sometimes this accuracy doesn't matter. For example, Lincoln's diagnosis was kidney cancer that had spread through his body to his liver, lungs, spleen and brain. He did not have an operation to biopsy his kidney to prove this was the case. Instead, his oncologist looked at his scans and decided it most likely started in his kidney and spread to the other affected organs. The way the cancer had spread indicated to him that Lincoln's kidney was most likely the place of origin. Therefore, a biopsy was not necessary. It would not have changed the outcome for Lincoln or his treatment and it may have been uncomfortable and unpleasant.

Understanding 'prognosis'

Your prognosis tells you how your illness is likely to progress. Most diseases are classified by stages. Knowing what stage you are at can provide information about how long you are likely to live, how you may die and what effect treatments may have on your survival time. 'Prognostic factors' tell you more about your prognosis and can be characteristics, such as age or other conditions. For example, a younger person who has the same illness as an older person may survive for longer because youth is on their side. Or a person with the same disease at the same stage may have other conditions that will shorten their survival time.

Lincoln was given a diagnosis of 'Renal Cancer Stage 4'. This meant the cancer had spread from his kidney to three other sites. There is no 'Stage 5' but given all the other places his cancer had spread to, he would have been a 'Stage 10' if they had gone that far. According to the statistics at the time of Lincoln's diagnosis, twenty per cent of these patients live for five years. Unfortunately, Lincoln would not have survived for that length of time because of other prognostic factors. His cancer had spread to four areas in his brain; one of these was just above the part that controlled breathing. These patients, like Lincoln, only have a five per cent chance of surviving twelve months. This means that ninety-five per cent of these patients are likely to die within twelve months.

Each case and disease is different. Your doctor will take all these factors into account and try to predict what will happen in your case. These predictions are based on years of medical research and experience, but can only be used as a guide. They cannot provide an exact time when death will occur.

Many doctors use statistics to help you understand what will happen. This is particularly true with a cancer diagnosis. You should be told about survival rates. If you are not given this information, and you want to know, then ask! The five-year survival rate refers to the percentage of people living five years from diagnosis, with the same grade and stage of disease. These figures can guide your future planning, such as applying for payouts of superannuation and life insurance or taking an overseas holiday.

Experience versus statistics

While statistics can tell you the likelihood of an event, such as approximate survival times, they cannot tell you *how you will experience* this process. In this I am reminded of the term 'qualia'. It refers to how we as individuals experience things at a personal level. We know people perceive pain, temperature and sensation in general, differently. Complex interactions between how your body works, your emotions, your upbringing and your cultural background will affect your experience of disease *at a personal level*. Although we may have a general idea about what being ill is like, it is difficult to predict how you will experience your end-of-life symptoms as an individual.

There are differences between what we think a person is experiencing compared to what *they* know they are feeling. This may be a factor in cases where your family would like to continue treatment but you would like to stop. Or when treating teams think one last treatment should be tried. Their intentions are often honourable, but they may be forgetting that your experience of these treatments and side effects is yours alone. Your response to treatments and side effects is your own unique experience. This means *you* need to make the decisions on *your* treatment and how to manage the side effects. Others cannot understand what you are going through except in a general sense. A starting point for me is to find out what the dying person wants and the reason for their decision.

Sometimes the dying person will talk to their carer to get support in decision making. Mac, a 75 year old man with a terminal illness, wanted to stop an experimental treatment. It had extended his life for eight months but had some very unpleasant side effects. Mac knew if he stopped the treatment his life would end in a matter of weeks. His doctor was reluctant to stop providing the treatment because despite the terrible side effects, it was working. Mac did not want to upset the doctor who had helped him access the experimental treatment in the first place, without which he would have died several months ago, but he still wanted to stop the treatment. Concerned his message was not getting through, he asked his daughter Liz to intervene. She asked me the best way to handle this situation. I referred her to my *Refusing active treatment decision-making guide* (see Chapter 3). Liz met with the doctor and Mac stopped the treatment. While there is absolutely no doubt his survival time was shortened, his quality of life (as he perceived it) improved. He died peacefully several weeks after his decision.

Seeing the bus that is going to hit you and end your life can make you do strange things, including pinching a beloved spouse in broad daylight to make sure you are not dreaming. If they clobber you back, you know it is for real. You know now there are less threatening ways to start believing this most devastating and catastrophic news. I have also explained how to work out what your timeline is broadly likely to be or when that bus may come along. The news you have is awful but you are not alone in this situation. You have a treating team and, I hope, some personal support. They can help you plan for the best death possible.

five things i know now

1. The news that you or your loved one is dying is hard to believe, but it does sink in eventually.

2. Managing family, friends and workplaces is exhausting. I should have delegated someone for this task.

3. The internet is wonderful but can contain some very distressing stories that may not be helpful. I stopped reading after a short while.

4. Your experience of your disease is yours alone.

5. There is such a thing as a reverse bucket list!

CHAPTER 2

getting the support you need

The Australian healthcare system is complex, rarely enjoys good press and horror stories abound, including some frightening dying stories. In my experience – and while there are definitely areas for improvement – when taken as a whole and certainly by international standards, our healthcare system is good. You should be able to get the support that you need.

I am confident to make such a bold statement. This is because to get the best death possible you rarely require highly technological, complicated care. In fact, such things may hinder a good death. Being allowed to die in a society that cannot cure death, but can do an awful lot to extend the process and make it unpleasant, can be harder than you think. One way to avoid this is to have a clear idea of the type of death you would like, and support to turn your plan into reality.

There are sections of our healthcare system that are best equipped to cater for those who are dying. I will explain what teams of people you need to help you, and the style of care that will provide the best death possible.

Palliative care

Palliative care is what the dying person needs at the end of life. It is an approach to care that is available to patients of all ages with any type or combination of diseases. This means that palliative care is available for those who are dying from any condition including heart disease, dementia or cancer. Palliative care recognises the patient is dying and provides help in managing this process, not just physically with end-of-life symptoms such as pain but also emotionally. A lot of time is spent in the palliative care consultation talking about you and your circumstances.

It is important to realise that palliative care is an *approach* to care that helps to provide comfort for all aspects of end-of-life care. It is used by a variety of healthcare professionals in different settings for patients who are dying. Carers are also supported through the dying process and afterwards.

Australia has an excellent reputation in delivering palliative care services. A key part of your end-of-life plan is going to be finding services that use the palliative care approach. Some of these will be dedicated palliative care services that have a team of healthcare professionals including specialist doctors and nurses. Alternatively, it may be your general practitioner (GP) who understands and wants to provide this type of care. Palliative care is also provided in large and small hospitals throughout the country. Some of these may have a dedicated palliative care unit – beds within a ward kept for that purpose – or a consultation service that works across a large hospital.

Accessing palliative care services

Your doctor should provide you with a list of palliative care services in your area. Not all doctors provide end-of-life care, but they can all refer patients to either a palliative care specialist or a palliative care nurse working in a home nursing or hospice service. If, for some reason, your doctor fails to do this, then request a referral, or contact your local home nursing service (check the telephone directory) and make inquiries. You may have to be persistent and hustle. When my mother was diagnosed with a terminal illness, we asked her surgeon to refer us to a local palliative care unit. The medical director of that unit had changed and it took us several phone calls to track down the current medical director, forward the referral and get an appointment. In Lincoln's case we used a local service recommended by our oncologist, which we approached ourselves. Our GP was not available to provide any after-hours services, so we stayed with the doctor who had diagnosed Lincoln. He understood the palliative approach.

The website Care Search provides excellent resources for dying Australians and their families (see Appendix 2). It is an online resource containing relevant and trustworthy information about palliative care, funded by the Australian government as part of the National Palliative Care Program.

Early access to palliative care extends quality of life and living time

My friend George is a 55 year old non-smoker who appeared well except for a persistent cough and increasing back pain. He thought his cough was due to asthma and his back pain due to a new armchair. Neither cause was correct. Instead he has Lung Cancer Stage 4, which has spread to his back and other places in his bones. He was given a survival time of approximately two years (if he had treatment), and a referral to an excellent palliative care team.

George embarked on a number of chemotherapy drug trials and was tested to see if he would benefit from the new immunotherapy treatments. After a while, none of the treatments were effective, but were causing problems elsewhere in his body and he was not suitable for immunotherapy. Meanwhile, the pain was getting worse and George had not yet consulted the palliative care team; in fact, he cancelled the referral. He thought starting palliative care meant he would die sooner and he wanted to 'fight' and stay positive, and as he was not yet actually dying this could wait.

I have heard versions of George's story many times and it always leaves me perplexed and frustrated. It is one of those cases where what I know as a researcher and an ethicist makes a difference to a good death. Going early to palliative care will not shorten your life! There are well-conducted studies showing that quality of life is improved and survival times may be increased. It is important to think positively when facing end of life but that should not prevent you from seeking out services that can work and have been shown to be helpful to the dying. Making contact with a palliative care team as early as you can is a step towards getting a good death in Australia.

Developing support teams

Two support teams work best. One is your healthcare team (palliative care aware is best) and the other will be your personal support group. Each will be dedicated to getting you to the end of your journey, according to your plan or wish list. Lincoln's journey was a relatively short one of four months. He had two small teams looking after him: myself on the personal side, and his oncologist and a visiting nursing service as healthcare support. Significantly, I had several people supporting me: colleagues visited me when Lincoln was in hospital, my sister helped with household tasks, a friend took me to meditation every week, another friend supplied pro bono grief counselling. Many friends from Bardon State School in Queensland helped take care of our daughter, Zoe. In fact there was another support team dedicated to Zoe, including a professional counsellor organised by Education Queensland to assist her in what was a bewildering time for an 11 year old. This was of great benefit to me and Lincoln. Brandon, our 21 year old son, relied on his friendship group.

Formal support systems

Depending on the illness you have and the length of time you have been treated, you may have a number of different doctors, nurses, and other allied health staff looking after you. Healthcare knowledge is expanding all the time and it can be difficult for one health professional to be an expert in all that is needed to treat a patient. This means, increasingly, that patients have a large treating team made up of doctors and nurses from different specialties and a variety of allied healthcare professionals. Keeping up with what each one is planning to do or doing on your behalf can take work.

Co-ordination may be a major issue for you and your carer. Ideally the carer needs to take on this role as they will know your wishes and plans.

Doctors

There is no need to change your medical team as long as they are comfortable with your care plans and goals. They need to be skilled in providing treatments and medications that treat the symptoms of dying. A GP who is experienced in palliative care or a palliative care specialist is great to have working with you but is not essential. Many physicians are comfortable providing end-of-life care across a broad spectrum of medical specialities. They are what I call 'palliative care aware'. It may be the case that your doctor does not wish to co-ordinate your end-of-life care. Do not be offended by this. Ask for a referral to a specialist in palliative care. Many home nursing services also know and can recommend GPs who have expertise in palliative care.

Nursing services

A home nursing service is essential for those who want to die at home or even those who wish to die in hospital but need care at home. Most home nursing services will have specialist palliative care nursing staff. These are highly trained in managing end-of-life care.

They can organise equipment, provide support and training for the carer, monitor and manage end-of-life symptoms, explain what is happening and how matters at end of life are likely to progress.

Personal care workers

These provide direct personal care such as assistance with showering, changing beds and eating. They should work under the direction of a registered nurse and can be employed by the home nursing service. Personal care workers are employed in a number of settings including nursing homes and some hospitals.

Psychologists and counsellors

Psychologists and counsellors can provide grief counselling and emotional support for the person who is dying, the carer, friends and family members. Many schools provide counselling services for students who face the loss of a parent or a sibling. Workplaces may also provide a counselling service.

Social workers

Social workers play a vital role as they can link you with a range of government and non-government healthcare services. They may also be skilled in counselling. Importantly, they advise on what financial support is available from Centrelink for both the dying person and the carer. We used our carer payments to offset hospital parking costs, which can add up quickly.

Community services

Most cities offer a directory of community services, sometimes at the front of your local telephone directory. Many of these are not-for-profit enterprises that can provide services such as delivered meals, assistance with housework and garden care.

End-of-life or death doulas

A relatively new kind of end-of-life worker is the death doula. Traditionally a 'doula' provides emotional and spiritual support for a woman during childbirth. Death doulas provide this service at end of life. They can work with you to help you make sense of the choices that are available to you, according to your values. They are becoming known in Australia for those seeking a non-medical, more spiritual (in the broadest sense) approach to dying. Death doulas are not a regulated health profession and arguably would not seek to be. If you would like to explore this option, go to the Australian Doula College website (see Appendix 2).

Informal support systems

Family and friends are clearly important during this very emotional time. Be prepared that some may be overwhelmed by their emotions and may act in unusual ways. For those who are facing death and who do not have many family or friends to call upon, community volunteer services may be available. Hospital chaplaincy services are also an excellent source of support. They cater for all religions including the non-religious. A local home nursing agency may also help you locate this type of support.

Carer support

Carers are without doubt the backbone of the Australian healthcare system. In 2015, the Australian Bureau of Statistics counted over 2.8 million unpaid carers in Australia who provide all sorts of care within the family home. Most often these are family members but they can also be friends or neighbours. In recognition of the work they do, the Australian government provides a small payment to carers through Centrelink. They also fund Carers Australia, which is an organisation dedicated to helping carers.

Carer burnout is a recognised part of informal care giving. If you are a carer, accepting as much help as you can, as early as possible, is vital for you and the person who is dying. When care needs increase, the amount of work required can seem daunting and carers are often emotionally burdened, as well as physically tired. Please consult Carers Australia (see Appendix 2). They provide many tips for helping to manage the carer role, including an information kit.

Support groups

These are informal groups convened by people with the same disease to provide support and share information. Your treating team will most likely know if support groups are available. If they do not know, an internet search should help you find one. Different groups offer different services. While some offer social support, others provide counselling and information sessions. Some use online chat rooms or email and offer links to resources. These options are great for those who wish to remain private, or who live in remote areas, or who are not well enough to leave the house.

You need to be careful about what you post online. The Australian government has produced an excellent booklet, 'Protecting Yourself Online', that can be accessed through the Downloads section on the Cyber Security webpage (see Appendix 2).

Other support groups may charge fees, or be supported by pharmaceutical companies who wish to promote their products. While this may not necessarily be a problem for you, it is a good idea to know how groups are funded. Carer support groups also operate in all states and these are funded primarily by the federal government. For a carer support group in your area, call Carers Australia (see Appendix 2).

The internet

As I explained previously, I carefully used the internet in two ways to help me understand and plan for what was happening to Lincoln. The first was to locate resources and information. Please take care to use reputable sources such as the established not-for-profit organisations and government sites I have listed in Appendix 2.

The second way I used the internet was to read others' stories and experiences, in the form of blogs, where people wrote regularly about their personal situation. From these I learnt how things progressed for other people with kidney cancer, what they did, and what worked for them. Other people's personal experiences written in these blogs may be a great source of comfort, and may provide you with important information as well. They can also be distressing, but you can be the judge of what works best for you.

Where are you going to die?

Dying at home

If asked, most people would prefer to die peacefully at home, surrounded by their loving family and friends. Dying at home is a wonderful ideal and is possible for many, as most Australians are within reach of a nursing service that visits the home and provides assistance. However, dying at home is resource intensive and you will need a strong personal support team including at least one carer, preferably more, to help as dying progresses.

Home nursing services do visit in most areas of Australia but the key word here is *visit*. The nurses may come once or (rarely) twice a day but they do not move in. The carer is the person doing most of the work to help the dying person. A carer is a family member or friend who takes on the responsibility of caring for the dying person. The nurse and the doctor give instructions to the carer to assist the dying person. In this way the person may be able to die at home comfortably.

If the dying person or their family has the funds, hiring a nurse is another option. This may be an enrolled nurse – with a diploma in nursing who is endorsed to give medications – or a registered nurse – these commonly have a degree in nursing. This is an expensive choice but can be useful if you have the financial means. It is best to hire the nurse through an agency so they can check qualifications and fitness to practice.

Dying in a hospice

This is my personal favourite. A hospice is a special facility that caters for dying people. This makes it a perfect place to die as it strives for a peaceful, home-like environment at end of life, with excellent symptom control. Unfortunately, we do not have many hospices in Australia. However, there are a few scattered around the country and it is well worth asking your GP if there is one close to you.

Dying in hospital

From a resourcing perspective, dying in hospital means that your personal support team of carers, friends and family can visit and not become exhausted from their roles as carers. While it would appear that large public or private hospitals may not be the best place to die, in many areas they provide excellent palliative care services. By their nature they are geared toward cura-tive treatment and moving patients quickly through the system. In the midst of this busyness, staff who are dedicated to palliative care – and there are quite a few who work in these situations – have to provide care in a setting that is straining to cope with routine surgery and emergency cases. Most do a fantastic job in difficult circumstances. Smaller hospitals that are public, private, run by a charity or based in a country town may be quieter and be able to provide palliative care. Some hospitals have dedicated palliative care units and the atmosphere is generally more peaceful.

If you do have a choice, check the availability of single rooms for patients who are dying. This includes public and private hospitals. Not all private hospitals have private rooms available. Many public hospitals have single rooms and these are often used for very sick patients or those who are dying. Having a single room is preferable and most hospitals will try to accommodate this if it is possible.

Dying in residential aged care facilities

If you are living in a nursing home or hostel, palliative care services should be provided on site. There is generally no need to move into another facility. However, the option of moving should not be ruled out if palliative care services are not available.

Working out your preferred option

We know that most Australians would prefer to die at home. I, however, would like to die in hospital or a hospice. I have seen good deaths both in hospitals and at home but I am comfortable in a hospital environment. Some of the more challenging deaths I have managed have been in the home situation where symptoms became unpredictable to manage or carers were exhausted from caring responsibilities. Plus, I live in a lone person household and have a very small extended family in Australia. Lone person households in Australia are predicted to grow from 2.1 million households in 2011 to close to 3.4 million households in 2036. Like me, these households may find it difficult to have enough carers to manage a death at home.

Planning for a good death means gathering resources to make sure your wishes can transform into reality. Everyone will have different requirements. If you are planning to die at home, you will most likely need a home visiting nursing service and some type of reliable home visiting medical support, such as a GP who makes house calls. Both of these are great to know about even if you plan on dying in hospital. A carer is essential in helping you manage your plans. Carers also need support. They should factor in some 'me' time and have a backup person in case they are unable to fulfil the role.

Your preferred option may not always be clear at the start of your journey, but should become so as you experience more of the options available for end-of-life care. It is important that you canvass a number of options and if you want to die at home you should have all the resources you need organised ahead of time, including having a hospital in mind in case your plans change.

five things i know now

1. Support groups can be a wonderful source of information and help.

2. Persistence is needed at times in accessing a service. You may have to 'hustle'.

3. Schools have counsellors who can help children face the loss of a parent or sibling.

4. Car parking at hospitals can be very expensive.

5. Carers need support too.

CHAPTER 3

developing a plan
for a good death

Planning to die well needs some thinking on your part – it is *your* death – and also requires that you communicate your ideas and wishes to your support teams. In my experience the way you live your life definitely shapes how you want to die. If you have not already done so, now is the time to reflect on those principles and values that have influenced your decisions and life choices. What does dignity mean to you? What are the things and moments in your life that have given you joy? What does quality mean to you in terms of living and now dying? What is beautiful for you?

The following process can be used to inform your decision making and end-of-life choices based on what has worked for you in life up until this point.

*1. Identify the values and principles
that you have lived by*

use these to

*2. Develop goals of care with your
healthcare and personal teams*

then

3. Put these goals into action.

Your death plan or wish list

The above three steps are the basis of your plan. It needs to be flexible, as the pathway to death can be unpredictable. This is a changeable situation, so perhaps we should call it a 'wish list' that is based on your values and goals. Your plan will outline the things you would like to happen at death, based on what matters to you in life. The goal of this book is to get as many of your end-of-life wishes realised as possible.

You may choose to write down your plan or it may be based on conversations. Lincoln and I spoke continually about what he wanted – a peaceful and pain-free death – and importantly what he did not want to happen – a lot of time spent in hospital. Perhaps you have already formed, and even voiced, an opinion on how you would like to die. Many people as they approach old age, or experience serious illness, will think about these matters. Early discussion is valuable, because it helps you clarify and communicate what is important in a less time-pressured and emotional environment. In these cases, you will be revisiting what you have decided previously, to see how and if this can now be achieved.

Defining quality of life

You probably don't think much about what 'quality' means in relation to your life until things start to go wrong. This was the case with Lincoln when he started having problems with his vision. A scan then confirmed four secondary cancer tumours in his brain. He could not watch television or read. He had to stop driving. At this point, we started to discuss death and dying. Quality, as we know, is an individual matter. For Lincoln, it was being in control, staying out of hospital, socialising quietly, thinking and talking and being organised. He was the list king! At end of life this translated into sorting things. Quite literally, he sorted through old boxes of things he had accumulated. It was almost like he was saying: 'What do I want future generations to know about me? What am I going to leave around and what don't I want anyone to know about?' I was not allowed to be present while this task was happening. It was a deeply private endeavour. This was another way of Lincoln being organised and staying in control: by deciding what would remain of his life afterwards.

When you have such limited time, the choices you make can become easier. What do I want to do in the time I have left? Where do I want to be? Who do I want with me? If this is difficult to think about, try reversing the questions. What do I never want to do again? Where do I never want to go again? Who do I never want to see again? Lincoln did not want to go to hospital. He hated it. He was offered radium treatment for the cancer in his brain and refused it because he did not want to spend his limited time in hospital and clinic waiting rooms being fitted for the necessary devices to help the procedure.

it is all about you

It is your own definition of quality of life that is important here and I mean *your* own: not your partner's, your parents', your children's or the treating team's but yours. You may consider others' opinions but at the end of the day it is what *you* want that counts.

These choices will affect your death, and your loved ones after you have passed. They may also help your departure be a lot more comfortable than if left to chance. I like the idea of quality as beauty. In this case, how beautiful do you want the end of your life to be? What constitutes ugly? In Lincoln's case a beautiful life was an active life, characterised by sport, done with like-minded friends with plenty of humour. It was a life of care and support for his family in a very practical sense. He did most of the housework, shopping, and ferrying of his children to sport and work. He was the great organiser of his family and his friendship group. He loved words, and often wrote amusing poems that were circulated to his fellow riders after a major event. He enjoyed reading biographies and watching sport on television.

His deteriorating eye sight had a great impact on his quality of life as he defined it. He could not read, could barely type, and watching TV was also a problem. His blurred vision was due to the position of one of his brain tumours and it did improve slightly with medication. Nevertheless, his sight, or lack thereof, became a very early erosion of his quality of life. He could not drive or help out with tasks as he had always done. This deterioration in his condition triggered further decisions about treatment or more precisely what treatments to refuse.

---

in order to make some decisions about your journey, ask yourself:

1. What is important to you in life?

The best death possible will reflect what you value in life.

For example, my friend John derives a great deal of satisfaction from work. He says he would keep working until he physically could not manage to do so. Lincoln disliked his work; it paid the bills. His focus was fitness. Quitting work after his diagnosis was easy. Quitting running was forced upon him because of his condition, but he rode his bike up until six weeks before his death.

2. **How are you going to spend the very precious time that remains?**

    Some people like to travel, visit friends or organise goodbyes. A few years ago, while en route to Sydney, I sat next to a married couple on the plane. We started talking about this book and they confided they both had terminal cancer. Neither of them had long to live and they loved to take cruises. They had sold their property and were going to Sydney to join a series of cruises. They expressed the wish to die while cruising or at least be brought ashore at the last possible moment.

3. **What treatments are you happy to continue and which are no longer worthwhile?**

    Although there are not many treatments available to Lincoln, he did refuse some that may have briefly extended his life but had nasty side effects or required lengthy hospital stays. These decisions need to be discussed carefully with your treating team. A point may be reached when therapies are no longer effective and may be stopped. This does not mean that you will not receive care – you will – but the goals of that care will be different. They will be about support and comfort as you approach the end of your life.

4. **Is it important to have as much time as possible or to have less but better-quality time?**

This will depend on your personal situation. For sole parents, accepting life-prolonging treatments for as long as possible, irrespective of side effects, may be important. What also needs to be considered is whether the extra time will be of sufficient quality to enable you to interact with family and friends.

5. **How long are you likely to be able to make your own decisions and is it important to stay in control?**

Despite our best efforts, as we approach death we may lose control and have to trust our care to others. These will be your healthcare and personal support teams with whom you have previously discussed and developed your goals of care, end-of-life plan and wishes.

Understanding 'dignity'

By dignity I mean respecting and honouring an individual as a human being. Every person has worth. All people are entitled to the highest levels of care. Each choice regarding treatment is important and needs to be respected. If you are dying, time spent thinking about what dignity means to you, and *what it looks like in practice*, is essential. It will be a reference point to help guide your end-of-life decisions.

In Lincoln's case he had a very clear idea of what dignity meant to him. He was a person who had exercised most days of his life. It gave him energy and a great sense of well-being. Lincoln's idea of human dignity was bound closely to his thoughts about quality of life, which was tightly woven to his ability to control his body and be active. During his end-of-life stage, he preferred to manage his own hygiene needs. Once he needed help to manage his personal care, such as support in the shower, he felt he was losing both his dignity and the quality of his life. I did not agree with him on this issue. I had seen patients, students and colleagues with a variety of disabilities for which they received assistance and never thought their dignity was compromised. However, it was not my idea of what constitutes dignity that was important here – I was not dying. It is the person making this journey who decides the route, not the passenger who is helping them reach their destination.

Respecting autonomy

Autonomy refers to a person's ability to make up their own mind and control their own destiny. In health-care we provide information and options for patients so they can make informed choices. Patients are free agents who are also able to find out information about their illness and research possible treatments. Patient autonomy is a very important part of health care and is reflected in the need for all health workers to gain consent for treatments from their patients.

A critical aspect of autonomy, from a legal point of view, is that the patient has to be of sound mind to make these decisions. The patient must have the mental capacity to understand the choices that are being put before them. If the doctor or treating team holds the view that the patient does not have this capacity, then the situation changes and a substitute decision maker – such as the next of kin – is given the legal authority to make decisions according to what the patient would want, or what are in the best interests of the patient's comfort and well-being. These issues are discussed in detail in Chapter 4, where you can learn how to ensure how your wishes are followed should you lose your mental capacity.

It is important that those surrounding the dying person do not become *paternalistic* – this means taking over the role as decision maker from the patient, as a father would a young child. In terms of your doctor, in order to avoid being paternalistic they are legally obliged to gain consent for treatment by presenting all the options based on their medical knowledge and to let the patient decide what to do for themselves. Doctors are not allowed to coerce a patient into making a decision and, crucially, neither is the family. For example, a GP may advise a patient to quit smoking because of the harmful effects of smoking on their health. The patient may choose to ignore this and ethically the GP must accept this decision. They will probably not like it and take every opportunity to persuade the patient otherwise, but at the end of the day the patient has the right to do what they want, and the GP should continue to treat them.

Paternalism or paternalistic attitudes can exist in families. My mother had not enjoyed good health for many years, experiencing a series of vexing problems. She thought carefully about her future health needs and decided to fill out an advance health directive; refusing active treatments should she lose the capacity to make her own decisions. She was very pleased by this and decided that my father should do the same thing. My father was in a different situation. Although 80 at the time, he was in good health, and he thought he might like to have some treatment, should the need arise. My mother, who was feisty by nature, was insistent this was wrong and that he should follow her example. She had been sick many times and she knew what she was talking about! I was called in to adjudicate. This was a clear case of paternalism on my mother's part, who – acting out of her experience – did not want my father to have treatments, which in her case had been unpleasant. Despite being married for more than 50 years at the time, she had to respect my father's position, which she did. Eventually.

Autonomy at end of life

For end-of-life treatment, the principles are the same. During Lincoln's last hospital admission he felt very uncomfortable. He had two problems. First, he was vomiting because a tumour was blocking part of his intestine. Second, he was becoming more and more short of breath because one of his lungs had started to fill up with fluid. He recognised he was close to death. He felt very weak and could not stand for long periods.

We were told his treatment options were: putting in an intravenous (IV) line for fluids to give the anti-vomiting medication quickly, and inserting a tube into his lung to drain away the fluid. He agreed to have the IV line, but not the lung drain. He did not see the point, as it was explained to him that the fluid would keep coming back to cause problems with his breathing. He did not want to prolong his life at this stage because his quality of life had deteriorated to what he thought was unacceptable. His doctor's response was to check that Lincoln understood what this meant. Death would come sooner – in a matter of hours or a day – rather than later – in a few days – with the option Lincoln had chosen. Lincoln understood this information and the consequences of his decision. He was alert and had the capacity to make this momentous decision. His doctor then made sure Lincoln was receiving enough medication to keep him comfortable.

Quality of life, as we have seen, is a completely individual matter. There is no right or wrong. There is just what you want, based on what the treating team can offer, in terms of good medical practice. Lincoln's lung could have been drained. He may have lived a few days longer in hospital, and he would have been very weak and most likely unconscious and therefore not in control of his bladder or bowels. In his mind, this would not have improved his life at all. It would not have returned his energy, allowed him to see properly or get out of bed. He could not eat or drink. He would be unable to participate in life with me and our children. Lincoln made me understand *his life* should not be prolonged where there was *no quality* in the sense that *he recognised*. We realised that we needed to be clear about what treatments he should accept, or I should agree to on his behalf.

Understanding futile treatment

Knowing when a treatment is futile, and should stop, is an important aspect of planning your death. Understanding this will help you get the best death possible. Treatments can be futile in two ways. First, they can be futile from a medical point of view; that is, they cannot achieve the desired clinical outcome. Second, they may be futile from a personal view. This means they are not meeting your needs or goals, despite working clinically.

When we watch programs on television about medical care and the treatment of illness, we are often impressed by what can be done to save lives or dramatically improve the quality of life. Many people know about, and benefit from, the advances of modern medicine. This makes it difficult to accept that, in some cases, there is no further treatment available to achieve a cure or prolong life. Even in these times of modern medical miracles there are limits to treatment, and the point is reached when active treatment should stop. The focus of care is now on the management of end-of-life symptoms to ensure comfort.

To assist in making the decision when to stop active treatment, or not offer a treatment, doctors rely on what they know to be 'good medical practice' for that patient and their situation. Where a treatment reaches the point that it is not offering any benefit, when it is futile or even causing harm, it should stop.

Doctors are not obliged to offer treatments they consider futile. However, in some cases patients or family members may demand them because they do not understand what their impact may be. I have heard of cases where people have been resuscitated against the physician's better judgement because family members have become angry and insisted. The outcome is usually poor with admission to the intensive care unit and life support withdrawn at a later date. In these cases we have merely intervened in the dying process, making it longer and more unpleasant than it needs to be. We cannot cure death but we can prolong it, and it can be most unkind, and not just for those sitting at the bedside.

While doctors are not required by law to offer treatments that are 'futile', as a patient or family member you can expect to discuss with your doctor why a treatment may be withdrawn or not offered. Towards the end of life most, if not all, treatments are stopped and the dying person is supported with comfort measures. Generally, but not always, these are not complicated and can be managed with assistance in the home or in a small hospital. This means that those who are having treatment far from where they live should be able to return to their home or a facility closer to their home.

Consent to treatment

You will recall that all patients need to consent to treatment. A doctor, nurse or your family cannot make you have a treatment, unless under special circumstances for those with severe mental illness. You also have the ability to stop treatment at any time. Many people at end of life will try experimental treatment to see if it works for them. They can stop it at any time. This includes being on a research trial that is testing a treatment. You are not obliged to commence or continue any treatment that you think is not in your best interests or according to your personal goals.

Refusing or stopping a treatment is likely to have serious consequences. You may die sooner. **It is critically important that you understand this and discuss all your options with your treating team and your family.** The decision to stop may mean that you transfer to another team skilled in palliative care. This will be a decision for the treating team and may be based on: how resources are distributed within the hospital or the health service, the type of disease you have, and the experience of treating teams with palliative care.

refusing active treatment
decision-making guide

1. Is the treatment working? If the answer is yes, you may want to continue but you are not obliged to do so.

2. Are there any 'harms' from continuing this treatment? What do *you* consider is a harm? Harms may be symptoms such as nausea but also may include the location of treatment. It may be keeping you in hospital when you would prefer to be at home, or in a city when you live in the country.

3. Is this helping my quality of life, as I define it, or is the treatment reducing it?

4. What is the opinion of my treating team? Do they think this treatment is beneficial? Why?

5. What is the opinion of my personal support team? Do they think this treatment is beneficial? Why?

6. Will this reduce or extend the time I can spend with family and loved ones?

7. What is the quality of the time I am likely to receive? Will I be able to talk or move? Will I have control of my bladder and bowels? Will I be able to recognise family and friends?

8. What supportive care is available?

Cultural requirements

If you have bought this book my understanding is that you are interested in dying well and obtaining the best death possible, according to your culture and religion. If you are unsure how to proceed with a particular end-of-life issue relating to your culture or religion, it is important that you discuss this with your cultural or spiritual adviser. Once you have this advice, tell your healthcare team so they can ensure that the care they deliver is culturally and religiously appropriate and not offensive in any way.

Developing your plan

Now you have considered some of these ideas, you can develop your plan with confidence. If possible, do this with your personal support team first, then take it to your healthcare team. Both of these groups will need to test whether your plan is feasible in order for your wishes to become reality.

Steps to developing your end-of-life plan

1. Think about what quality of life means to you. Write three things that are important in your life and how you would like to manage the time remaining.

2. What is a 'good death' for you? Who do you want there? Do you want music playing? Do you want your pets, friends and family present?

3. Develop a bucket list (things to do before you kick the bucket) or, as Lincoln did, write a reverse bucket list (things that you will never do again).

4. Think about your preferences for visitors. There may be people you never want to see again and that should be respected.

5. Write some broad care goals or a care wish list.

6. Deal with legal requirements (see Chapter 4).

7. Identify and include any specific cultural or religious requirements you would like to observe.

8. Discuss your goals and plan with your personal support team. Is this feasible in terms of the support others can give?

9. Discuss your goals with your healthcare team. Ask them how they can help you meet your goals. Identify who else you may need to bring onto your team.

10. When you have worked out what support is available, decide on your preferred location for dying; is it at home, in a hospice or in a hospital?

11. Develop an action plan for use in times of emergency. This needs to be clear and workable. For example, if you rely on home oxygen or other electrical devices, make sure you have a backup plan. Summer storms in Australia are notorious for interrupting power supply.

12. Enjoy life! You now have your death plan sorted.

If you are not sure how to start, think about what you do *not* want. For example, I do not want to die in hospital; I do not want to have pain; I do not want to be separated from loved ones. Communicate your plan to both your personal and healthcare support teams. Lincoln's plan looked like this:

PRINCIPLE	IMPLICATION AND ACTION
Quality of life over quantity of life	I want to avoid being bedbound, incontinent or unable to make my own decisions.
Manageable pain and discomfort	Actively monitor and manage pain via: medication, meditation, application of hot packs and use of hot baths.
Promoting the best life for our children	Clear and timely explanations according to their age. External support as necessary with counsellors. Encouraging normal routines and friendships.
Staying fit	Modified exercise program including weights, rowing machine, bike riding and walking.
Death at home	Home nursing service and medical support organised. Preferred hospital identified.

Getting the help you need

Now that you have a better understanding of your end-of-life goals you can work out the services you require. Revisit the previous chapter where I explain what is available in detail. You may decide that to meet your goals you need a:

- supportive GP who is able to visit the home

- palliative care or home nursing service

- palliative care specialist doctor

- hospital that can appropriately manage complex symptoms

- carer and a backup carer

- counsellor, chaplain or social worker.

Shifting the goalposts

Most of us experience plans that do not work out for all sorts of reasons. Lincoln and I had faced many challenges previously that required us to be flexible. We learnt early in our married life not to set anything in stone, and we became adept at changing course when we needed to, depending on the circumstances. End-of-life care is very similar. The course can be unpredictable, and you may find that you change your goals several times. For example, in true Lincoln and Sarah style, our goal of Lincoln dying at home was not met. The course of his disease meant that he chose to go to hospital to manage his end-of-life symptoms.

Being flexible

Good communication skills are useful at every stage of life including negotiating end-of-life care. It is important to develop an open line of communication between your personal and healthcare teams. Your wishes facing death can change and that is completely understandable. Flexibility is the key. For example, you may decide to have active treatment and then change your mind and refuse. It may be that some of your choices and preferences are unrealistic, so you will need to be open to advice about what can be achieved. Take time to think about what is important to you in terms of goals of care. Review these with your treating and personal support teams. Are they workable? Can they be achieved with the type of illness that you or your loved one has? Are they legal? Euthanasia is illegal in Australia but this situation is being challenged, depending on the state or territory in which you live.

For this final journey, find your own path. Think about your goals of care, write these down and discuss them with your treating team, your family and your religious advisers, if appropriate. Develop your plan. What would you like to do? What do you want to happen? What support will you need personally and professionally? Remember, Australia has an excellent healthcare system and palliative care professionals will help manage your end-of-life care. A good death for you or your loved one is achievable in Australia.

five things i know now

1. Quality of life is incredibly personal. I would still give a great deal to have Lincoln back for a while – in any condition – but that would not be his choice and that must be respected.

2. Plans need to be able to change to suit the medical circumstances. Lincoln died in hospital and not at home as we originally thought. Develop a plan 'B' and be prepared to use it.

3. Knowing when to stop treatment is an important part of getting a good death.

4. Treatment harms may be medical, social, or related to geography or culture.

5. Cruise ships have morgues!

CHAPTER 4

the legalities

According to folklore, at the end of life the patient is told to go home and put their affairs in order. Often this means attending to financial matters and completing or locating their last will and testament. Now that you have worked out what you would like your death to be like, these documents can be more meaningful and personalised. I am not legally trained and I cannot provide legal advice. Instead, I speak broadly about the sort of legal documents you may find useful and some tips about how to locate the best forms for your circumstances.

Australia has a number of different states and territories and each of these require slightly different forms. The intent is the same: to provide guidance and instructions to others for health matters when you have lost the ability to do so (advance planning documents), or when you have died (your will), or to nominate a person to make financial or health (or both) decisions for you when you cannot.

If you have not done this already, I recommend you do it as soon as possible following the news you have a terminal condition. This is because you must be of sound mind to fill out these documents. Illness can be unpredictable and you may deteriorate suddenly, or there may be a delay in processing or locating documents. Lincoln and I had trouble tracking down the wills we each made 22 years ago when we married.

We had a copy with our documents at home but were told the original version was needed. We had left that with the solicitor for safekeeping. Having no prior knowledge of such matters, and not thinking we would need the will this early in our married life, we had put it out of our minds. When the time came to produce the original copy, we found the solicitor's firm had amalgamated with another firm, which we then had to track down. The Law Society in Queensland keeps a record of who merges with whom and we were able to find the new firm that had the original copies of our wills. It was a huge relief to know these were still in existence and we did not have to make another.

A person's last will and testament comes into effect once they have died. The best way to write a will is to work with a legal officer. A public/state trustee (see Appendix 2) will provide this service at an affordable rate, or you can use a local solicitor.

There are other legal documents that are of great benefit in planning end-of-life care prior to death. These set out your healthcare instructions in advance should you lose the mental capacity to do so. They are often called advance planning documents. You can also nominate a person to make decisions on your behalf once you are unable to make them yourself. This person is called a substitute decision maker. They do not have to be a relative – they can be whomever you nominate as long as you use the correct document. Unfortunately, these documents are named differently according to where you live. You need to find the correct forms for your state or territory.

Alzheimer's Australia has a number of helpful planning tools available on their website, including information in many languages, sections on how to make your plan, and advice on the correct type of form to use (see Appendix 2). It has been established to help people with dementia, for whom these documents are especially important, but the documents and the processes are useful for everyone. Some states only use particular forms that have been specified in legislation. This means some documents are not necessarily recognised in other states or territories. For example, Queensland has particular documents that you must use for your decisions to be honoured by a court of law in Queensland. These are the advance health directive and the enduring power of attorney.

Remember: while you are of sound mind you should always be consulted about treatment decisions. Your advance planning document only comes into play when you no longer have the capacity to make decisions.

What decisions can I make in advance?

The forms generally record whether you would like to be given life sustaining measures in the event that you have lost the mental capacity to make this decision. Life sustaining measures include cardio-pulmonary resuscitation, assisted ventilation (breathing on a machine), the administration of antibiotics, tube feeding and intravenous fluids. You can also specify if you would like to donate your organs, your corneas or your body tissue – such as bone – after your death.

Who do I tell about my documents?

It is a good idea to lodge your advance health planning documents and decision-maker documents with as many people as possible including your GP, trusted family members or friends. If you are regularly attending a hospital, lodge one there as well. If you already have one of these documents, it is best to review them every two years as your condition changes.

Financial issues

If you have a superannuation policy, and most Australians do, or a life insurance policy, it is worth checking with the policy administrators to see if you can access these funds early. In some cases where the death of a person is expected within twelve months, you may be able to apply to have the funds released to you as the dying person. Your doctor will have to certify this is the case and it will have to be approved by the company or organisation involved. If you are in this position, these additional funds may be very useful in paying for aspects of your end-of-life care, depending on your requirements.

Euthanasia

The word euthanasia is derived from a Greek word meaning 'good death'. Generally, it is understood to mean the practice of *intentionally* ending a life in order to relieve intractable (untreatable) pain and suffering. The word intention is important here as euthanasia sometimes gets confused with the practice of giving high doses of pain relief at end of life. However, to be euthanised means to be given medication that is *intended* to kill you. That is the *intent*. Once dead, your intractable pain and suffering stops. In the other case, large doses of a pain reliever is given and a person dies. Here the *intent* is to relieve the pain and the death is secondary. Due to the nature of the drugs we use this may shorten the dying person's life, but not always, and the intention is not to kill the person but to relieve pain.

At the time of publication euthanasia is illegal in Australia, although a few states are attempting to change the law to make it legal. Should these states be successful, my understanding is there will be strict conditions around who can be euthanised. There may also be more discussion from the Australian Medical Association who recently indicated they remain opposed to euthanasia. While the ability to precisely control the timing of your death is one of the attractions of euthanasia, one can time death in many cases at end of life by refusing treatments that extend life, refusing fluids and food – which are often not required or wanted anyway – and pain should be able to be controlled as well. Modern medicine has a virtual arsenal to treat pain. Palliative care physicians are trained in this area and we also have a specialist medical faculty in pain medicine as part of the Australian and New Zealand College of Anaesthetists (ANZCA).

The ability to be able to end your life precisely, at a time and place of your choosing, is seen to be a fundamental human right and justified ethically as part of being an autonomous individual who wishes to make their own decisions. This reasoning has underpinned the legislation in other countries. There are, however, safeguards that the Australian public and political representatives need to examine and these concerns are usually considered when developing the law that will enable euthanasia to take place.

Chief of these concerns is the idea that a vulnerable patient may decide to be euthanised because they feel that they are a burden to their family, or the family are pressuring them in order to inherit their assets. The patient must also be of sound mind and be able to state the reason why they want to be euthanised. This means patients who have a terminal condition that may affect their mental capacity are not likely to be eligible to be euthanised, and this would include patients with advanced dementia.

My understanding is that the legislation proposed in Australia is likely to contain the safeguards mentioned and insist that you have to be: of sound mind and not being coerced by family or friends, terminally ill with death expected within a specified time frame, and experiencing intractable pain or suffering that cannot be relieved. Nevertheless, for those who have explored all other options – and you are going to be forced to have considered those – and who still wish to be euthanised, it may be an option in the future in Australia.

Let us now consider three cases of people at end of life to establish who may be eligible for voluntary or active euthanasia *if* it were decriminalised in Australia.

This first is the death of a man who was, by all accounts, in agony and close to death. He may be eligible if his pain was unable to be treated effectively, he was of sound mind and he was not being coerced. The second is a beloved father who took three days to die. He was in a nursing home, he had dementia and had stopped taking fluids. This was extremely difficult for the family to watch and their agony was real, but the dying person was pain free and appeared peaceful. It is likely that he would not be eligible as he was not of sound mind and was dying peacefully. The third is Lincoln's death, where active medical interventions were stopped, the end-of-life symptoms were treated, and life ebbed away in a process I have seen so many times I have truly lost count. Lincoln would probably be ineligible as he was able to get good pain relief and symptom control.

Getting your house in order legally is an obvious and important part of end-of-life planning. Advance care and power of attorney documents that come into effect once you have lost capacity are available throughout Australia, but are different in each state and territory. Check the website provided (see Appendix 2) or ask your local solicitor to help you locate the correct documents and fill them out properly. Once these have been completed, make multiple copies and keep them handy for distribution to the hospital you intend to use, all of your health team, your home nursing service and your personal support group.

five things i know now

1. Taking care of financial and legal matters should happen as soon as possible after diagnosis of a terminal condition.

2. There are different documents and procedures required in each state and territory of Australia so make sure you get the correct documents.

3. Legal firms can amalgamate and take your originals with them!

4. It is useful to have a copy of your advance planning document with you and lodge it with every health facility you use.

5. If euthanasia becomes legal in Australia, there are likely to be safeguards to protect the vulnerable people in our society.

CHAPTER 5

dying 101

After we accepted the news that Lincoln was going to die, he became curious about the process. What would happen to him physically as he went on this final stage of his journey? Would it be really awful? Would he be able to cope? How would the family be involved? These types of questions are normal. Dying has become a process much removed from everyday life. There are many people who have not witnessed the death of another person, or seen a dead body. Now is the time to answer these questions and describe what generally happens in the last hours of life.

Reviewing your goals and plan

By this time it is likely that you have decided where you want to die. Like the rest of your goals, this needs to be flexible and worked out in consultation with both your healthcare and personal support teams. It can be a tiring and difficult process for loved ones to take care of a dying person at home. Not all carers feel able to manage this and their wishes also need to be respected.

There may be other reasons why death at home might not be possible. This was the case with Lincoln. We had discussed with the hospice service our wish for Lincoln to die at home. They had indicated that they could do this unless his intestines became blocked by the tumours that were all through his abdomen, in which case he would have to go to hospital for supportive therapy to assist him to die comfortably. Unfortunately, this turned out to be the case. When Lincoln's lungs and abdomen swelled with fluid and he found breathing increasingly difficult, we proceeded to the hospital that had been the site of a number of his previous treatments.

We were fortunate that an individual room became available and we moved there to commence the final leg of the journey. Lincoln's death followed a pattern I had seen many times. He became drowsy until he was not able to speak anymore. He seemed to be asleep. He had not eaten anything for two days, having only a few sips of water and ice chips to suck. He began to breathe in a way that was like snoring. He would take a series of breaths and then there would be a pause before he took another breath. The pauses became longer and longer. During this time I would wait for him to start breathing again. This type of breathing is known as Cheyne-Stokes respiration and is common at the end of life. Eventually, the pause becomes permanent and breathing stops altogether. The family gets used to waiting for the next breath as the pauses get longer and longer until, finally, it does not come. The person stops breathing, their blood is no longer circulating around their body and their heart has stopped beating. At this point, the person has died.

Body changes that precede death

A rather old-fashioned word that means 'to be approaching death' is 'moribund'. A person who is moribund or close to death will become sleepier and talk or respond less. This does not mean they cannot hear you, so you can keep talking to the person or play their favourite music. Other people nearing death may become confused and restless. In these cases, medication may help the person to be more comfortable.

Generally, the person will not be eating or drinking. Ice chips, if they can be managed, and keeping the mouth moist with a clean, wet cloth or sponge will help the person stay comfortable. The amount of urine decreases and a loss of control over urine flow and bowel movements may occur in some cases. When this happens, incontinence pads may be fitted for comfort.

Breathing patterns will change and may become noisy in the way that I described previously. The dying person may become quite cool to touch – particularly their hands and feet. These may become blue-looking. This bluish colour may also be visible on the face, particularly around the nose and mouth. Fever may be present and can be alleviated with cool sponging or medication.

How long does it take to die?

Recently, I heard of the death of an elderly gentleman with advanced dementia who was confined to bed. His family made the decision to stop his antibiotics and the intravenous drip that was in place was no longer required. The son of the dying man was telling me his story. He was very upset it had taken three days for his father to die once the drip had been removed. I was not particularly surprised – it can take some time for a person's body to slowly shut down and die. I was more concerned that no-one had apparently explained this process to the family and they thought it unusual and cruel.

If we haven't seen someone die we are likely to form our opinions from the media. When we watch a person dying on the television or in a movie, it is usually sudden. In real life, it is often a much slower event. The length of time it can take is unpredictable and this can make things very difficult for families who want to stay with the dying person. They can become tired and anxious and may have to leave because of other matters beyond their control, such as work or care responsibilities. Sometimes people just want the death over with, to put themselves and perhaps the dying person out of their misery. As the carer you should prepare yourself: this may take time, it is normal and you may want to have someone supporting you. This time-honoured process of saying goodbye is both desperately sad and sacred and the timing can be unpredictable.

Comfort measures

For the dying person there is much that can be done so they are not suffering. Cleaning the body, mouth care, and regular positioning and massage to prevent pressure areas (or bed sores) should be performed by the carer or nursing staff, but not necessarily registered nurses (see Appendix 1 for a list of who is who in the nursing world). Sometimes the eyes become dry or the ability to close them properly may be lost. In this case eye drops will keep the eyes moist. Wounds should be dressed to prevent any leakage or odour.

A fresh and comfortable bed should be maintained with clean linen that is changed when soiled. A special mattress may be required. These can prevent areas of pressure building up on the bony parts of the body. The room or bed area should be kept free from rubbish and any spills of urine or vomit should be cleaned promptly.

When the person is close to death it is time to review treatments once again. While turning, positioning, washing and feeding are all possible and may be required if the dying person is uncomfortable, when death is very close many of these types of comfort measures can be stopped. This gives the family uninterrupted time to spend with their loved one.

Administration of medications

These will depend on the symptoms present but can be given to ease suffering such as pain, confusion or excessive secretions. A combination of such medications may be required. These will be ordered by the treating doctor and given regularly by the nursing staff or the carer. In most cases at end of life this should be as often as is needed. If you feel, as the carer or as the dying person, more is required then speak up and let the nurse or doctor know.

The management of pain

The desire to have a peaceful death, free from pain, would be high on most people's end-of-life goals. The management of pain at end of life will depend on the type of illness and the overall health status of the dying person. There are many ways to manage pain, such as the application of heat or cold, meditation, massage, acupuncture and medications. All of these can be tried and may work together in a complementary fashion.

Sometimes very large amounts of pain relievers are required and family members may worry that the dying person is becoming addicted, or that death is being hastened unnecessarily by such large doses. I'll give you an example: Julie's brother Mathew was dying of cancer. He was addicted to drugs before he became unwell. On his last admission Julie told the palliative care team his history of drug use. They were glad to know as Mathew's pain relief did not seem effective. They increased his doses steadily to relieve his pain, until it was triple the usual amount required. He died peacefully.

While you can expect that doctors will help relieve pain you cannot ask them to end your life. This is called euthanasia and at the time of this publication it is illegal, although this may change in certain states of Australia in the near future. If a doctor, relatives or friends assist with ending a life in this manner, they may face legal consequences (see Chapter 4). This does not mean that you cannot have large doses of pain-relieving medication at end of life. This was the case with Mathew and Lincoln – who also had large doses of morphine as he was slowly being choked by malignant fluid infiltrating his lungs and abdomen. What is important here is to consider the *intent*. The intent must be to relieve pain, not to end the life. Sometimes the amounts required will have the unintended consequence of shortening a life but this is not the intention at the outset.

This is a complex and emotional area. I have consulted on cases where physicians have been reluctant to prescribe pain relief because they do not want to kill the patient or be accused of euthanasia. I have observed nurses who do not want to give pain relief, even though it has been prescribed, for the same reasons. Doctors are able legally to prescribe medication that nurses can give even if they know it may shorten a patient's life, providing there are sufficient clinical signs and symptoms to indicate this is necessary. This does not constitute murder or euthanasia. The intent must *always* be to relieve the pain.

Personally and professionally, I believe no-one should suffer a painful death. We have the means to alleviate pain and if the dying person requests pain relief at end of life, this should be given until the pain is relieved. They may well become addicted (as they are dying I consider this the least of their worries) and the medication may hasten their death. This is likely to be by a short time and the other option – that the dying person survives for a little longer in terrible pain – cannot be justified ethically or clinically. If you as the carer feel more pain relief is required, then speak up. You may need to be persistent.

Some dying people choose to take less pain relief medication as they want to stay conscious or less 'dopey', so they may interact with their children or their family. This is their choice and must also be respected. One of my research colleagues told me of a case he had during his palliative care rotation. It involved a young man dying of bowel cancer. He asked to leave the hospital, where he had been for a few weeks, and head to the coast to surf for the last few days of his life. My colleague, a junior doctor at the time and the same age as this patient, thought this may be okay. He was worried about what the patient would do regarding his pain, as it was likely to increase. He knew the patient was competent, checked he understood the risks in terms of his pain management and allowed him to be discharged. The young man left for the coast and returned via the emergency department some ten days later in absolute agony. My colleague was called to admit him back to the ward. He was shocked at how much pain this fellow was in. He could barely touch him to put in the intravenous line and administer the medication. When the pain was under control, the patient thanked him for that last opportunity to experience life, and died peacefully about eight hours later.

Staying with the body

You may want to stay with the body once the person has died. This is not unusual. Dead bodies are not usually unpleasant to look at. The deceased has stopped breathing, has no pulse and no circulation. They very often look peaceful. There is also a sense that the deceased body is just that – a shell of the former person, as the spirit or essence of that person has left the physical body.

The death of a person must be certified by a medical practitioner. If this occurs in a hospital or a residential aged care facility, the staff will arrange for this to happen. If it happens at home, a family member will have to contact the nursing service or the deceased's local doctor to issue the death certificate. The funeral company can then take the body away to their premises.

Depending on where and what time the death has occurred, you will be able to spend some time with the deceased. This is highly variable and intensely personal. I recall one case where a young wife found it very difficult to leave her husband's body. She remained in the hospital next to his body for six hours. I did not stay long with Lincoln's body. As far as I could see, he had gone. His body looked like a shell and knowing his dislike of hospitals I guessed his spirit would not be hanging around!

five things i know now

1. Dying people may be prepared to put up with more pain than we think they should.

2. Relief of suffering, such as being at the beach instead of being in hospital, is just as important as the relief of pain.

3. Some people may require a lot more medication than others.

4. Carers may need to alert doctors and nurses if they feel more pain relief medication is required to make the person comfortable. Be persistent.

5. Staying with the deceased person can give great comfort to loved ones.

CHAPTER 6

troubleshooting

The care standards you should expect

After 30 years of teaching, researching and working in health care I know not all care giving proceeds smoothly. Leaving aside the many reasons why problems may occur, it is useful to know:

1. What you can expect in terms of your health service.

2. What you can do if things are not going according to your plan or wish list.

In my role as a clinical ethicist I hear of times when end-of-life care is not optimal and the family or the treating team are distressed as a result. This can happen with any type of service provider, from your specialist medical practitioner to a hospital or a visiting nursing service, hospice or residential aged care facility. Sometimes this may be the result of unrealistic expectations on both sides, but not always.

For example, things did not go well for Val or her dying sister Janice. Val is telling this story, graciously reproduced here with her permission. You may find the following account distressing.

I went to see Janice in the hospital in the city on the Thursday before she died. She had some friends there and we were talking and laughing like there was nothing wrong. When it was time for me to leave, Janice asked if she could speak to me alone. She told me she wasn't sure how long she had to live and could I go and get our parents from the country town where they lived. Janice was insisting she wanted to go home one more time so she could tell her 16 year old twin daughters that she didn't have much longer to live. The doctors didn't want her to leave the hospital but she insisted and went home to tell her daughters, returning to the hospital later. The next day I dropped our parents at the hospital. Janice seemed her happy cheery self that day and the Sunday. On the Monday we went to the hospital and my sister was asleep. My niece told me she hadn't really woken up properly and everyone including the nursing staff thought she was tired and just resting. I left my parents visiting and when I returned I knew something was really wrong. Janice was very groggy and not really 'with it'.

What we found was a hideous situation. Janice was so out of control, tossing and turning and trying to get out of the bed even though she wasn't conscious. Her 16 year old twin daughters were trying to hold her down and at the same time trying to talk and tell her that we were there to see her. We all tried to take some time with her but I doubt she would have even known we were there. I tried to insist with the nursing staff that this couldn't possibly be right and could they please do something about it. It was met with a very vague 'yes they would' but I believe nothing was done until much later, when another shift came on.

We were all devastated. She would have hated to be in this situation. She was the sort of person who was very much in control of any situation and certainly would have done her utmost to get something done if it was one of us.

After a sleepless night we awoke to find she had made it through the night and we decided to go back up to the hospital. When we arrived, thankfully Janice was calm and peaceful. We sat with her for the morning, with nursing staff coming in and checking on her on a regular basis. Every now and then she would breathe like it was her last breath. This breathing was happening more often and towards early afternoon we knew the end was near. So it was with one of these last breaths that she passed peacefully away. Unfortunately the moment she passed away her phone rang. They had put a phone call through to her room so I had to tell one of her friends that she had just passed away. It was two weeks short of a year since she had been diagnosed.

Lessons learnt

From Val's story about her sister Janice, you can see that healthcare staff can get it badly wrong. When I heard about this case my heart sank. I felt overwhelmingly sad that Janice's daughters had to manage what appeared to be an episode of 'terminal restlessness' – where the dying person can become confused and agitated. Clearly, the nursing staff did not respond in a respectful or timely manner.

The question is: *what can you do about it?* Sometimes we are expecting too much, or more than what is possible given the dying person's condition, or the facilities of the hospital. It is awful to be having end-of-life conversations in a busy four-bed ward, as I witnessed some time ago when I was a patient and the woman opposite me was told her cancer had returned and there was nothing more to be done for her. Sometimes there are no alternatives. You will be able to judge yourself whether this is the case. In the meantime, let us consider what is reasonable to expect. In terms of care standards in any healthcare facility or at home, you can expect that:

All nurses, doctors, social workers and chaplains, regardless of their qualifications, treat their patient with empathy, respect and basic human kindness.

Healthcare facility standards

Most hospitals work on a rotating eight-hour shift basis. The morning shift is generally from 7 am − 3 pm, the afternoon from 3 pm − 11 pm and the night shift from 11 pm − 7 am. These are approximate times. Some hospitals also use twelve-hour shifts or shorter periods of duty. Medical staff should check the patient daily, but more frequently if the patient deteriorates and medical assistance is required. The registered nurse will be able to judge when this is needed.

For each shift a nurse is usually assigned a number of patients whose care they are responsible for delivering or co-ordinating. It is likely you will have a different nurse daily and it helps to find out who is in charge of your care or that of your loved one. This is the person who should be able to update you on the status of the patient's condition and what to expect.

In Janice's case, her condition had deteriorated and professional assistance was required immediately. Additional medication may have helped keep her calm and prevented such a distressing situation for both the family and Janice. The family were aware of this and that is why they asked the nursing staff for help. Having been alerted, the nursing staff could have contacted the doctor and reported the problems. The doctor would have reviewed the situation and ordered the medication if needed. The nursing staff would then give the medication. Sometimes nursing staff are reluctant to 'bother' the doctor. In this case, as a private patient, I would offer to ring the doctor myself and explain the situation. If you are a public patient, then ask to see the most senior nurse on the ward, relay your concerns and ask for a medical review of your loved one (see Appendix 1 for an overview of nursing hierarchies).

Respectful communication

All healthcare facility staff should introduce themselves. If they fail to do so, then it is a good idea to take the initiative and introduce yourself and tell them what is important for you and your loved one. Start by introducing yourself and thanking them for doing a good job in what are often difficult circumstances. Then mention your key goals.

For example, 'Hello, I am Sarah, Lincoln's wife, thank you for taking care of him today. We are very keen to keep his pain under control. Can I let you know when he seems to be uncomfortable?' Or, 'Hi, I am Val. My sister Janice has been very comfortable here but she seems confused and angry today. Is there anything we can do to help her? Would some extra medication be useful?'

What would be nice but cannot always be delivered

Some facilities may be able to provide a private and well-appointed room with after-hours meals and good coffee available and consistently helpful staff. We used three different hospitals and one stood out in terms of the physical environment and the quality of the staff. Lincoln felt safe in this facility. Interestingly, it was the least well-known of the hospitals but it really suited us. The staff knew end-of-life care very well. They listened to us. The car park fees were capped at a set amount. The car park attendant got to know me and if I was very upset and the parking bay was tricky he would park my car!

End-of-life care is a difficult area to work in and it is acknowledged that not all staff are at their best every day. Some are agency or relief staff who are new to the hospital and may be trying to get used to the ward processes or layout. Some may be working overtime because of staff shortages. My heart always sinks when I hear of nurses working the dreaded double shift. It is definitely not good for them and I would suspect it's not the best for their patients either.

Dealing with care issues at the ward or unit level in a healthcare facility

If you have concerns about the care that is being provided, there are a number of ways you can address this immediately. At one hospital that Lincoln attended there was a problem with hygiene standards. His dressing had leaked on the sheet and the staff did not change it. I poked my head out into the corridor and noticed that everyone looked very busy. I scouted around and found a clean sheet on the linen trolley and changed it myself, but then there was no place to put the dirty sheet. We rolled it up and put it in a corner of the room. It stayed there for two days! On the third day Lincoln placed it at the door of his room so staff would have to trip over it when they entered. Then it was picked up. This standard of care is poor. I asked to speak to the charge nurse. I was told she was too busy. Then I asked to speak to the assistant director of nursing in charge of quality standards. The charge nurse then found time to hear my concerns and she was very understanding.

Once you get to speak to someone about your care issues, you need to think about what you are going to say and how you are going to say it.

Having difficult conversations

- Try to keep conversations friendly, even when you feel things are not going too well in terms of the care being provided. In my case I asked the nurse at the desk several times if I could speak to the nurse in charge but no-one followed up with me.

- While you may feel intimidated, that may not be the intention. It could be staff are extra busy or feeling out of sorts.

- Avoid broad statements and focus on specific concerns using accurate information. For example, I said: 'I would like to speak about my husband Lincoln's soiled bed linen. It is on the floor and I do not know where to put it.' The answer was: 'You mean bed 23?' I replied: 'Actually, I mean my husband Lincoln Winch and yes I believe he is in bed 23.'

- Try to be positive and look for ways you can work with staff to meet care goals. In my case, I had changed the sheet. I just needed to know where to dispose of the soiled linen.

- Acknowledge that staff may be busy. Ask for a time when you can speak to them. Be persistent.

- Try to find out how things work in the ward. Ask who is in charge of the patient's care for that shift. I did find this difficult to track, so I would write it down to make sure I knew who I was speaking to, and who I needed to contact if there was a problem.

- Give staff an opportunity to speak and explain what may be happening in the ward. There may be staff shortages, but this should not mean that basic care standards deteriorate.

- When problems occur ask staff what they think will work and what you can do to help. When my mother, who had a terminal illness and dementia, was in hospital following complex surgery, the staff gave her a bell to push if she needed help. Unfortunately, she was confused and did not know how to use it. I asked the staff how they were going to keep an eye on her overnight as she was too confused to use her call bell. Once they realised this they explained that they would check on her regularly.

- Try not to take things personally. Instead, bring the conversation back to the facts and the goals that you are trying to achieve.

- Most importantly, if you are feeling upset, practise the conversation with a friend before holding the real one. I find this very useful. This is an incredibly emotional time. You want the best for your loved one and if you are like me you will be tired, sad and angry. Sometimes words don't come out the way you want them to, or you are not sure what to say. In this case it helps to have rehearsed your request with a friend or relative or even aloud to yourself in private.

- If you do feel you are unable to have these conversations, perhaps someone else can do it for you. Most of us have a fearless friend and this is a great time to call for their assistance.

Dying at home

Care in the home is very different to care in a hospital. For a start, the carer will do a great deal of the work such as keeping the room clean and comfortable. It is beneficial to work with a home nursing service. They employ nurses in all categories who come to the home and help manage the care of the dying person.

What you can expect from the home visiting service

- A full nursing assessment and a plan of care that incorporates your goals.

- A 24-hour contact number in case of emergency and an emergency plan. This may not be the actual service that comes out in the night but you need to know what to do and where to go if you have a problem at 3 am.

- A regular pattern of visiting based on your particular needs.

- The visiting nurse should be respectful of your property. And you should ensure a clear and safe entry to your home.

- The service should provide a window of time when the nurse will be visiting, for example in the morning or late afternoon. This enables you to enjoy other activities during the precious time you have left. You do not want to be waiting all day every day for the nurse to arrive!

- Advice on how to organise your home so that care can take place easily.

- Advice on how to manage care so you as the carer do not hurt yourself.

What would be nice but cannot always be delivered

Home nursing staff visit your home but most often can only stay for a short while as they have a number of patients to see. It is also difficult, given the number of patients they have to see and the unpredictable nature of the care they have to give, to provide a regular or definite appointment time. While you should get some idea of when the nurse is coming, they cannot always guarantee a time because they are not always sure what they will be called upon to do during their visits.

Getting organised with equipment

Visiting home nursing services often have equipment that can be loaned or hired. You may also choose to purchase products that may make caring easier, particularly in terms of pressure relieving mattresses that prevent pressure sores. During the course of Lincoln's illness he suffered quite severe skin breakdown. We treated it with a number of dressings but his skin became very thin and tore easily. Dressings and equipment can be sourced through a home nursing service, a pharmacy or by buying direct from a supply company.

Using emergency departments

Managing difficult end-of-life symptoms that emerge unexpectedly may mean a trip to your local emergency department. These can be located in public or private hospitals. We had to do this with Lincoln on Easter Monday 2008. Our doctor was away and Lincoln's lung started to fill up with fluid. It was also in his abdomen. We went to the emergency department of our backup hospital to have the fluid drained. The emergency physician had not seen Lincoln before and listened while Lincoln laboriously told him about his symptoms. Scans were ordered to confirm what was happening. When these came back the doctor called me into another room where the scans were on the viewing box for discussion. He seemed surprised by the extent of Lincoln's disease and felt there were enough clinical signs to commence a morphine infusion to 'put this poor bugger out of his misery'.

I think I can count the times on one hand when I have been lost for words. This was one of them. I managed to say, 'Thank you for considering Lincoln's pain needs but you (the doctor) need to have the conversation with Lincoln' (who had just huffed and puffed his way through the explanation of his symptoms). At this point the doctor just left, presumably to see someone else. I went back and told Lincoln what had been said. He decided to continue with treatment and requested the fluid be drained.

Since this time I have had the occasion to work with emergency departments and I realise how this may have looked from this doctor's perspective. He did not know Lincoln, or me, and perhaps thought the request for drainage of the malignant fluid would be futile. That was not a bad call; the fluid did recur reasonably quickly. The next time it happened Lincoln did not get it drained; he started a morphine infusion and died shortly thereafter. I still think this doctor could have spoken directly to Lincoln about the results of his scans, but maybe he was having a bad day. I was angry about the lack of respect shown for Lincoln's autonomy, but I don't think Lincoln noticed. He was concentrating on breathing.

If you have to visit an emergency department, take your advance health directive with you. Speak up about your goals for end-of-life care. The emergency physician is not likely to know your case. Be prepared for a potentially unfiltered objective opinion. I have since discovered that some emergency physicians have training in palliative care and many emergency departments are striving to offer excellent end-of-life care.

Escalating concerns

Complaints are taken seriously in health care. When you enter a hospital or sign up for a service, a brochure or fact sheet outlining the complaints process should be given to you. Put this in a safe place with your other documents. Hospitals have staff members dedicated to addressing complaints ranging from the quality of the meals to poor nursing or medical care. If the complaints are serious they may be followed up with other authorities. If you are not satisfied your complaint has been addressed properly, you can contact the Consumers Health Forum of Australia, which represents the concerns of healthcare consumers – that is, patients. It also has a fact sheet on making complaints (see Appendix 2).

Changing teams or doctors

Sometimes communication breaks down to an extent where it is best for all concerned to change teams including the treating doctor. This is not to be embarked upon lightly; it takes energy and time when you may not have much of either remaining. However, it may be a consideration if you feel you are not being listened to, or the treating team are disrespectful or even disinterested in your needs. If this happens to you, the best way forward is to arrange a final meeting with the doctor and:

1. Ask for a referral or a summary of your treatment. You may be charged a fee for these documents.

2. Take a second person with you and take notes of the conversation.

3. Try to remain polite. You do not have to explain why you are changing your team.

4. Take your treatment summary and your goals to your new doctor.

Working with healthcare staff to get the best care

It is my absolute belief that most healthcare staff try to do the best they can every day. Sometimes they have a bad day, they are too busy, the equipment they need does not work or is not available, they are tired from shiftwork or they too are suffering a personal crisis. All of this is understandable.

If you are the carer or the person who is dying your tolerance for poor care, or bad behaviour from those who should know better, is likely to be low. In these cases you are entitled to try to get the best you can for your loved one. How you do this is important as you really want to make things better, rather than worse.

five things i know now

1. Some nurses still refer to patients by bed number. This has to be corrected – every time it happens. Your loved one is a person. Not a number.

2. Practising difficult conversations will help you feel prepared.

3. You must speak up when care is below standard. Making a formal complaint can improve the care for everyone.

4. Emergency departments are working to improve their contribution to dying well in Australia.

5. A fearless friend can help you when things are not working out.

CHAPTER 7

reflections on grief:
don't leave home without
your sunglasses

A confession

While Lincoln was alive I had decided to prepare for grief by using traditional academic methods. I bought books; I read the academic literature. The books were on my bedside table and Lincoln remarked on them, asking: 'Do you think you will be okay?' 'Of course I am not going to be okay,' I replied. 'I am going to be a soggy, devastated mess (a somewhat accurate prediction on my part) who is going to get on with it.' Others coped and so would I. There were the children to think about. Lincoln agreed, stressing I should continue to exercise (he wrote me a weights program) and walk, and listen to a playlist that he would put together for me. We agreed this would be a great plan. I am a dreadful cook and was somewhat concerned for my future eating possibilities – he wrote out some recipes and bought me a whole range of hand implements such as cup measures and handheld juicers. He cleaned out the garage and called me down for a quick lesson on how to use various tools that he thought would come in handy. We had recently moved into a high-rise apartment and it was agreed Zoe and I should stay there as it would not be too much for me to keep clean. (Lincoln had done all the cleaning, as well as the cooking and the washing!)

We tried to think of every eventuality. I would be sad, but was not to cry too much. Instead, I should celebrate the good things and remember all the laughing, walking and talking we had done over the years. Plus, I had the children. He would go to some sort of afterlife and wait for me there. He did not have any religious beliefs, but we found it comforting to think we may meet up in the future. He said that may end up sooner than I thought if I didn't learn to control my workaholic tendencies, find something to laugh about and enjoy life.

Looking back now, several years after these conversations, a few things stand out. Having a plan is great, being practical is important and prioritising what to take care of is critical – such as putting the children first, making time for physical fitness, keeping up with friends. What we did not plan for was for what we did not know: the profound emotional response to grief.

On the day after Lincoln died, I put on the playlist, turned on the music and walked across the road to head to the gym and start my exercise program. I had just crossed the road and was walking towards the gym when I could not walk any further. My legs would not work. Tears started streaming down my face. They would not stop. Next thing, I had collapsed and was lying on the verge, my face planted in the dirt. I lay there momentarily overcome with anger and embarrassment. How could things move forward if I could not even put the first part of the plan into action? I got up and removed the earphones and felt better. My legs started to work so I returned home immediately in case anything else unexpected happened. I was still annoyed. What if the children had noticed? Had anyone seen me from the balconies of our unit block? Was I losing my mind? How was I ever going to manage without Lincoln if I could not go for a walk by myself without collapsing in a sodden heap?

I phoned a friend. She is a psychologist, an academic and a person who had lost her partner suddenly in tragic circumstances. She suggested I try walking without the music, tune the car radio to a talk station and prepare myself that I may not be listening to music for some time. Music reminded me powerfully of Lincoln who had a comprehensive and eclectic collection that he played whenever he could. Listening to music can affect the emotions in powerful ways.

The unpredictability of my tears made me realise that I should never leave home without my sunglasses. I could be out and about and hear or see something that reminded me of Lincoln and suddenly I was bawling. It could be in the supermarket aisle passing by his favourite type of orange juice, or walking along the street and seeing a bunch of bike riders, or going to the gym. It was incredible how many tears came out of my eyes during those first few years. I took action and changed gyms and supermarkets and avoided the places we used to go. I learnt to keep my sunglasses with me so if I started to cry I could put them on quickly.

Grief and loss

My understanding of grief is very much related to my personal experience; it is not an area of my professional expertise. While we don't tend to talk about grief that much, there is actually a lot of support available. Some home visiting nursing services, hospices, support groups and associations offer assistance with how to manage grief and what to expect. In addition there are a number of supportive organisations that can help you manage grief that can be accessed wherever you live in Australia. These are beyondblue and Lifeline. Their contact websites, specifically relating to grief and loss, are listed in Appendix 2. The beyondblue site includes an excellent fact sheet that can be downloaded.

Before Lincoln died, I was prepared for the fact that I would be very upset; I just did not realise how that would translate physically. Immediately after he died I kept on with my usual tasks but they took much longer to complete. While I slept very well, others have problems sleeping. I had trouble eating all through Lincoln's illness and afterwards, so I lost weight. Others find eating a comfort and gain weight. Your immune system can become weakened during the acute grief phase and you may find that physically you are more unwell than usual.

Some folk find they are feeling better in a year, others (like me) take longer. My understanding is that while everyone's responses are different, *grief is a process, not an event.* This means it takes time to adjust to your loss. While those feelings may never entirely go away, you should reach a point where they do not continually dominate your thoughts and feelings. You do need to be as gentle with yourself as you can be, as your circumstances permit.

There are some symptoms that you need to investigate promptly. These are suicidal thoughts, ongoing problems with sleeping, or an inability to complete the usual tasks of daily living. If you feel things are getting on top of you, act quickly and see your GP for guidance and help.

I had huge adjustments to make: becoming a single parent, an adult child leaving home for overseas and supporting my mother through her death. I started a new position ten weeks after Lincoln died. In retrospect this was foolish, although I did work part-time for the first twelve months. The first year after Lincoln's death was a completely wretched time, made bearable by wonderful friends, new and old. Some of our oldest closest friends no longer wanted to keep up contact after Lincoln died. In some ways I cannot blame them; he was always great company and I was a miserable mess. Despite this, I managed to make some new friends who were okay with sudden tears and had similar interests such as going to the movies or talking politics or, even better, combining both! They never knew Lincoln and surprisingly I think that is a good thing.

Taking care of yourself

After my spectacular episode the first day after Lincoln died, I managed to pick myself up and dust myself down (literally) and keep going. I began a regular exercise routine and found it very beneficial. I started thinking about the first version of this book and gained a contract with a publisher, which ended disappointingly. I think grief can make you vulnerable. You need to be more careful about who you trust and be alert to those who may wish to take advantage of your vulnerability. It is good to have a wise and trusted friend who you can speak to about situations you are not sure about. That is a truism in life, but more so when you are bereaved. Particularly if, like me, your trusted wise person is the one who has died.

Getting out and about

Following Lincoln's death I decided to accept every invitation that I was offered. This turned out to be a good thing for me. Some invitations dried up but others arrived. Despite how I was feeling – and most of the time I would have preferred to stay at home – I went out and mixed with new people, made new friends or caught up more regularly with older ones. My motto was, and still is, if someone can take the trouble to include me in their plans then I will accept. Some folk realised how difficult this was for me, particularly in the early days, and would often come and collect me to make sure I was getting out and doing something other than work. One of my new friends from this time has told me that over the years, as I have adjusted to widowhood, she has seen my hair become progressively blonder and my clothes brighter, reflecting my improved outlook on life.

Building a memorial

Lincoln had few instructions on what to do with his body after he died. He had thought an affordable option would be to put him in the wheelie bin to be disposed in the usual weekly garbage pick-up. I vetoed this idea on the grounds of workplace health and safety for the garbage collectors. His other request was that he did not want any religious references. He was agnostic (meaning he was not sure there was a God) and he had not changed his mind when he became ill.

One of our shared passions was walking through cemeteries. We found them utterly fascinating. Toowong Cemetery was a particular favourite and I secured a plot on 14th Avenue, buried Lincoln and then waited for over two years to decide what to build to celebrate his life. It seemed such a final thing to do and for a short while after he died I wondered if the whole thing had been a bad dream and he really was alive, just hiding, ready to surprise me. He had been a great practical joker. This time there was no-one to pinch me in case it was a dream. It was real. He was in that grave and I needed the memorial to be perfect. It is. In one of those absolute quirks of fate I was fortunate to meet one of Australia's only freemason architects, Pete Macfarlane. Actually, it is now Dr Pete Macfarlane – his doctor of philosophy studies were on building non-religious memorials.

Lincoln's memorial is part of Dr Pete's PhD and is called 'Love Always'. Pete, his partner Mandy and I created a wonderful, protected, sacred space that blends in with the surrounding older graves. The outer protective curve is concrete and the wavy inside seat is covered in sparkly ceramics. The structure is a metaphor of why I love Lincoln so much. He was somewhat reserved on the outside and then an incredibly sparkly personality once you got to know him. He was absolutely dependable and sturdy and I just so loved to talk to him about anything and everything. When I sit or lie on the seat, the curves surround me and it feels protective and super private. The space invites conversation and contemplation and I go there often; it is peaceful and beautiful. I can now listen to his playlist and tell him my news. Others also visit and sit and chat for a while – he is a great listener, although I miss his witty replies. There is a bike tube there as well!

five things i know now

1. Never leave home without your sunglasses.

2. Grief can make you vulnerable to exploitation by others.

3. Building a memorial can be therapeutic.

4. Funeral architects exist.

5. Love survives death.

final thoughts

Is a good death possible?

Is it possible to die well in Australia? I think so. Being prepared helps and this book shares techniques and information that works. A combination of easy-to-access knowledge and skills should help you succeed. Understanding the language – prognosis, diagnosis, and futile treatment – is helpful and learning how to navigate your way around the health system to find palliative care is important. Think through your values. How have you lived your life? What is important to you generally, in a religious sense or culturally? Consider your resources. Do you live alone? Do you have family members or good friends who can support you? What type of disease do you have? What will work best for you?

When you have thought about and discussed your plan, then identify the correct advance planning documents for your state or territory. If you experience a care difficulty during your journey then speak up: be respectful, but stand your ground and persist. Enlist the help of a fearless friend if you feel that you cannot do this yourself. You may need to change teams or take your complaint about poor behaviour further for your sake and for others. This is a sad, emotional and difficult time made more bearable by thinking, planning and finding support. Take care of yourself as the carer and keep to your goals and values as the dying person.

This is your death, your final act and you can be the director.

It has been many years since that awful day when Lincoln, aged 48, was diagnosed with terminal cancer and our lives changed forever. I have moved from the city, renovated an old cottage in the woods and moved back to city, slowly transforming into a platinum blonde wearing garish clothes (or so I am told!). Lincoln's weights are now used as doorstops. Brandon has married beautiful Emma. Zoe is finishing university and has a fabulous and fun partner, Tom. Every year the Ashgrove Rangers Running Club hold a memorial handicap race in Lincoln's honour.

It has not been easy without Lincoln in my life. I am not going to lie to you. I believe in truth telling, which is just as well, given that I work as an ethicist. Occasionally I think I should have pleaded with Lincoln to have one more treatment in that last 24 hours of his life. If that malignant fluid swamping his lungs and abdomen was drained just once more, he would have survived for perhaps another 48 hours. Then I could have been with him just a little longer. After all this time, I would still give a great deal to have him back – just for a day. Clearly, this is about Sarah, not Lincoln. He recognised he was at the end of his life and could not continue. There was no way he would ride, run, joke, eat or drink again. He knew that. The following sounds exceptionally trite, but it is true. I needed to love Lincoln enough to let him go when he was ready. I did, but it was so very hard. Lincoln taught me much about life and, as it turned out, death. I learnt how to truly respect another's wishes when they so violently clashed with my own. I sure do miss him.

Throughout our relationship, Lincoln and I had many plans and dreams. Some became reality, others, such as surviving into old age together, were not to be. Our last plan is the one I have shared with you in this book. He had a peaceful death. He left this world the way he lived it – with humour and dignity, on his terms. If you or your loved one is facing the worst possible news, I trust this book goes some way to help your journey be the best it can be. I hope, like Lincoln, you have the best death possible.

New York, 2007

APPENDIX 1

nursing hierarchies

There is a nursing hierarchy that is present in most hospitals and although the names may change, it will roughly be like this:

Assistant in nursing: this person has very little formal training and should only perform very simple tasks that do not require a good deal of supervision.

Student nurse: training in a university-based degree program to be a registered nurse or through a TAFE college to become an enrolled nurse.

Enrolled nurse: qualified with a diploma in nursing from a TAFE program or from a previous hospital course. Some have special qualifications so they can give out simple medicines.

Graduate nurse: just graduated as either a registered nurse or enrolled nurse.

Registered nurse: experienced nurse who has undertaken at least three years of study usually from a university, but may also have graduated from a hospital-based program from some years ago.

Advanced clinical nurse: a very experienced nurse usually in a speciality area such as palliative care.

Charge nurse or Unit manager: senior nurse who manages the care of a particular unit.

Assistant director of nursing or Director of nursing: a senior nurse who manages a number of units or a particular area, such as the medical division or the education section.

Executive director of nursing: the most senior nurse in the hospital who has responsibility for the overall management of the nursing service.

APPENDIX 2

useful websites and phone numbers

Alzheimer's Australia
Website: www.fightdementia.org.au/planning-ahead

Australian Government Cyber Security
Website: www.ag.gov.au/RightsAndProtections/
CyberSecurity

Australian Doula College
Website: www.australiandoulacollege.com.au

beyondblue
Website: www.beyondblue.org.au/the-facts/
grief-and-loss

Carers Australia
Website: www.carersaustralia.com.au
Telephone: 1800 242 636

Care Search
Website: www.caresearch.com.au

Centrelink
Website: www.humanservices.gov.au

Consumers Health Forum of Australia
Website: www.chf.org.au
Telephone: 02 6273 5444

Lifeline
Website: www.lifeline.org.au/get-help/topics/loss-grief

Medical Dictionary
Website: www.medical-dictionary.thefreedictionary.com

MedicineNet
Website: www.medicinenet.com/medterms-medical-dictionary/article.htm

Palliative Care Australia
Website: www.palliativecare.org.au

Public Trustees Australia
Website: www.publictrusteesaustralia.com